T0208449

i wish i wouldn't have survived

poems of my childhood

Mee Eun

authorHOUSE·

AuthorHouse™
1663 Liberty Drive
Bloomington, IN 47403
www.authorhouse.com
Phone: 1 (800) 839-8640

Published by AuthorHouse 03/10/2020

ISBN: 978-1-7283-5082-0 (sc)
ISBN: 978-1-7283-5081-3 (e)

Print information available on the last page.

This book is printed on acid-free paper.

dear joseph, i don't know.

the question still remains: what happened to me last night.

i'm teething on my childhood.

the moment i was born everything i ever knew was ripped away
from me and.

now i'm left trying to raise myself.

i don't know how to write a poem about this without it feeling like i'm scraping my knees against the asphalt. it's not that i haven't tried it's just that i've died every time all over again and that's just who i am. undead and undead and undead.

when a child isn't held, isn't comforted like she should be, she spends her whole life paying for it.

guess i'm being swallowed up by it, just like i always have been. skinny me was born on the side of the highway or maybe on the cold tiles of a kitchen floor, born covered in filth. and now i'm just some kind of bruised fruit. painfully overripe, it's a miracle my skin isn't melting off. bugs come and pick off pieces of me but i'll never be fully gone. always some pit to be left behind, rotten to the core. what i'm trying to say is, if you cut me open i don't know if you'd see juice or blood. i've always just felt like something to chew on.

when i was four i kicked and screamed when my mom tried to drop me off at preschool. not even goldfish crackers were enough to bribe me out of hiding behind her legs. when i was twelve i sang a song in italian for the talent show. mom bought me a sparkly blue dress and it ripped when they announced my name during the award ceremony and i ran onto the stage. when i was seven a girl named elizabeth invited me over and we played with dolls. i couldn't find one who looked like me but i didn't mind. the skinny ones with blonde hair and blue eyes seemed prettier to me, anyway. when i was five a lady i had never met before brought me into a small room at school and asked me to play with bubbles. she told me she knew my brother and i told her i loved my brother very much. when i was nine i hid in the bathroom during lunch and counted the ants on the floor. when i was fifteen i had a boyfriend whose sister was friends with my brother in middle school. she was killed in a car wreck. when i was seventeen i agreed to go to my first stay-away camp in california. i cried the entire plane ride, clutching both of the arm rests, reciting the prayers my parents taught me as a child over and over in my head. when i was thirteen elizabeth and i danced to teenage dream while jumping on my bed and her smile looked like the sun had bent down and kissed her between both her ears. when i was one day old i was ripped from my mother's tender arms and placed in a cold crib with white sheets. that is where the detachment began. ten fingers and ten toes and no soft body to label as someone who belonged to me.

i know it's late
& i know i should just go
i-
i just can't get the feeling of your skin off mine.

i'm no good at assessing damage,
there's
nothing i can say,
i know.

i just feel like
if i
keep you here
in this
space between the
take-off
& the
crash & burn,

maybe you could
find a way to
bring yourself
back to me.

maybe you could
find a way to
pretend like
i'm
what you want.

room above your garage. in a navy floral skirt my mom bought me for my birthday and you rip it off like a band aid. i say i'll scream and you tell me your father will come. what will i do then. i don't know. so i bite my tongue and watch the spiders in the corner of the ceiling. you're hitting me and i don't know why. my face is turning pink and the worst part is you think i like it. the word "no" is lodged in my throat and it's all my fault,

god.

all my

fault.

want to see my bones
'cause
he never got to touch them.

want to see a me
he never got to touch.

i want to live long enough to see the sun again. you know what i mean; the heaving isn't always easy. i try to sit in the back of the room so that no one will ask me my name or how i feel. or what i think or why i'm bleeding all the time. the thing i remember the most about childhood is the way my best friend's little sister's hands felt under the crashing waves when i pulled her out from the underside of the dock. choking. spitting. like i had pulled her out of the hellfire. grabbing. pulling. and somehow i knew exactly how that felt. burnt in the lungs. coughing up salt and sea glass. maybe it was my mom, maybe it was the stormy nights locked outside in the rain. sand and broken beer bottles. pounding on the door and. no one's coming. maybe it was my appendix. swollen. angry. needing to get out of me, need to get out. i don't know how to stop my brain when it decides to hurt like that again so. choke. spit. grab pull pound and. still. no one's coming.

figurine of an angel with paint peeling off of the cheeks. buried in the dirt and left to rot away like a dead animal on the side of the road with a *get well soon* balloon tied to its wrist. only wanting to be put to rest. only wanting to sink fully into the earth and find sleep. been like this for fourteen years. [nobody chooses to become a ghost.]

somedays,
i am made of dirt and sand and spit.
and the gates at the back of my throat
are wearing thin.

eyelids made of paper and
my heartbeat is everywhere but
in my chest.

somedays,
i wonder how god could make a creature as ugly as this.

somedays,
i think it wasn't god at all.

growing up mom loved to pretend i wasn't there. would call her name and ask her things and sometimes even scream and cry. she never flinched. i guess it was a way to punish me. it sure worked.

and the other thing it did was teach me how to be a ghost. i started to question what i saw in the mirror. if it was real and if other people could see it. i started to fear that maybe i had disappeared altogether. that maybe i had died and didn't even know it.

i guess a part of me did feel like it had died. like she had taken a stick and scratched me off the face of the earth. it stung like the harsh chill of winter on my baby-white skin. sitting out in the snow i watched through a window as life inside went on without me. how important could i have been if forgetting me was so easy.

you climb out of bed you see stars you wake up on the floor there are ants crawling on your legs your hair clumps out you step on the scale you step off the scale you drink water only to vomit you climb into bed you close your eyes you see red you feel your heart beating but it's lodged in your shoulder you climb out of bed you see stars you wake up on the floor there's music playing but no one else is dancing your mother's crying they ram the tube down your nose and you can't scream anymore there's cotton between your teeth you drink water only to vomit your hands disappear you step into the shower the water is hot like fire you step on the scale you step off the scale you roll the berries between your fingers to reduce the calories you check the numbers once twice you add a hundred and twenty four [just to be safe] you climb into bed you close your eyes you can't find god you choke on tears you scream for your mother but she left she couldn't bear to see you like that the window's open but you don't have the strength to close it you wait for the darkness to come you climb out of bed you see stars you wake up on the floor you turn your phone on silent you step on the scale you step off the scale you punch a hole in the wall your knuckles bleed you ignore your teacher when he asks you questions you ignore him again when he runs after you down the hall you walk home you taste blood you look in the mirror you see everyone you ever knew who died staring back at you through your eyes you limp to bed you wait you wait you wait you fear climbing out again because you believe the cold may just kill you you drink water only to vomit you close your eyes and

there is god. he's come for you at last.

but jesus christ, it's beautiful. that hollowed-out, sunken in, dead girl look. the way your knuckles look whiter than snow, the way your hair clumps together in the shower drain. the way it feels to go just one more day, one more hour, one more minute. the way the lights look when you stand up in math class and all of a sudden the people around you have turned into stars. the taste of fake cherries and blood. the never-ending cold. the warmth that only comes from other people, warmer skin.

and most days i think i would really still be prettiest that way. it's hard to grow into a body that i feel like i didn't choose. if i fainted now i don't think anyone would know what to do. i don't think they would even try to catch me.

ugly child. heaving underneath the bed. runny nose and bloody scalp, no urge to stop the bleeding. rotting. useless. piece of trash. lifting her up by the shoulders, shaking her until she seizes. *stop talking. stop talking. shut up. would you just shut up already.* she still cries when you strike at her. she won't learn how to swallow down the tears until she starts fifth grade. stupid brat. ungrateful bitch. filthy pig. burden. needy. waste of life. what can you say. she's eight years old and still wets the bed. [not your fault. her brother touched her, not you.] dirty little disgrace. nothing but a problem. pathetic, unlovable. [honestly] better off dead.

my brother and i were kids with little toy guns and he ran right up to me and shot me in the eye. didn't flinch. and it swelled and burned and stung and my mom said i should have been more careful, should have seen it coming. i hid under my bed and scribbled in my diary, then tore out the pages when i imagined mom and dad finding them. my brother burst through my door and i was nowhere to be found. and i started to wish it could always be like that. even if people came looking for me. that they would never ever find me.

i guess
heaven's real
just

not a place for
people like
me.

in my stomach i am sick and soft. i don't know which caused the other. it's a bad day to be afraid of the dark. cold and unrelenting and overflowing with an unbelievable stillness. lemon peels are sucked dry. too heavy to rise, too light to sink. too much of a child to even know how to swim.

i didn't do any of it right. no one would notice if i locked myself in the bathroom for weeks and let myself rot away. my body didn't ever leave that house i'm still there i don't want anyone to find me don't come looking for me [i don't have to ask for that though, no one's searching anyway.] when i close my eyes i see the back of joseph's head. and i know i want him to turn around i want him to. see me.

in fifth grade i learned how to turn myself inside-out. the first time i had to bite down on my tongue to keep from releasing the demons from my stomach who were rising up in my throat. [and boy did it bleed.] if god did one thing right when creating me [if it really was him] it was making me quick to learn. now i sit in crowded lecture halls or on the end of bus-stop benches and peel back the skin from my collarbones to my ribcage, unflinching as i undo my entire physical existence. if you're wondering what happened in fifth grade, so am i. the only clear memory i have of that year is my teacher reading us a book about a dog and running out of the classroom, choking and spitting, crashing into the walls we taped our art projects up onto. that was the year i was sent to see the old woman in the office behind the library, and when she asked about my family i stopped talking and every bone in my body felt like it was turning into water. that was the first time someone told me that it was safe to speak. i knew better than to believe her. [and i still know better now.]

remember when we used to lay in the dark and count the stars.
and how you would tell me that god knew them all by name.

i miss the time in my life when i felt like more than a bruised fruit.
i miss the time in my life when i felt like more than a soft body, a
fall-away eyelash, an afterthought.

isn't that what tenderness does to us, though.
seeps in through the cracks and buries us alive.
rips away at our flesh and dismembers us like the rotting gums
we are.

god used to know our faces but now we're blistering with cavities.

i'm sorry. i'm sorry.

i don't know how to explain this and everything is getting caught up in my throat but what you saw isn't what you think it was and i don't remember what happened, i really don't, i think it was just an accident.

they take good care of me, i promise. i swear.

i want to write poetry as good as the coffee i'm drinking. like a dry-high and four-in-the-morning on the side of a freeway looking out over the vacant parking lots and sleepy towns. towns made of paper and broken glass. the things mom and dad would fight about. the things they would break over each other's heads. we're still hurting and nothing's changing. we never grew up. washed away and crying ourselves to sleep.

life as a ghost: i don't cross my fingers anymore and maybe you're the reason why. i can't bring myself to wish for things i know could never happen, wish for things only real girls can have. it's the three-in-the-morning feeling of a phone call, blurry vision and apologies through sobs. it's the grave of the dog in the backyard with the cold rocks sitting on the fresh dirt. weeds and flowers pulling through like sins and forgiveness. it's you and your hands that everyone will see as soft until it's just you and me and they become fists colliding with my cheekbones.

and then you'll say you're sorry, gentle like always, because that's what you really are, you're really just gentle. i'm not a real girl and i know how the world works. you taught me how it is, keep teaching me how it is, and it's not just the night that's dark for me anymore.

there are real girls. and then there's me.

abandonment and i are no strangers. the thing about a parent leaving is that even if they come back, in a way they're gone forever. as soon as they step foot out the door a part of them never comes back. and that's all i see when i look in the mirror sometimes, parts of you and parts of me that you took with you that i'll never see again.

and you hoped i would forget.
and i still know them all by name.

how to: keep breathing when all you taste is metal and blood. water doesn't sate, just drowns. sleep is nothing but a surrender. your head is no longer full of flowers. only numbers and pounding. where did the good girl go. your head turns but only because your neck is snapped. you open your mouth to speak but nothing comes out. and it's all over but the rotting, decaying.

we bruise and we heal. we bruise and we heal. we bruise and we heal [and no one asks questions.] we trust bad men to teach us to be good girls and in the end when we are skin and bone we are finally proclaimed pure.

joseph tells me i'm running a fever and i tell him i'm running away. i'm a good girl now, i promise, and there's warmth just ahead but it's not for me.

i'm curled up on the floor of the shower. crying because i don't know if i'll ever feel warm again.

the last days on earth look like the decomposition of queen blue. watering down a bruise until all that's left is pale flush. the streets are empty and there is no music playing. dreams are filled with mom throwing herself from the seventh story of a building because she just. couldn't. handle. me. anymore. and my hands don't leave the concrete. and my fingers don't stop tracing the outline of her landing. there are no mornings without fevers. at night i lie awake listening as my heart beats almost as fast as everyone left. the last days on earth look like eyes wide open on the mortician's table. she stops. she sees me. and then she bleeds me dry anyway. [and god, i am so grateful for it.]

it's the morning after and i wake up with a sob still caught in the crook of my neck. someone wrapped me in a blanket, as if that would mean anything. animals aren't meant to be swaddled. but maybe that's not how they see me. maybe they look down when they're done and see a newborn, covered in blood and sweat and tears. i don't know when i fell asleep. i just remember dreaming that i was an angel and that god had finally taken me away from this hellish wasteland. i didn't have a body anymore and i think that might've been the best part.

dear god, i just want someone to be gentle with me.
to wrap me up in the shyness of the morning.
to kiss my blistering cheeks until the skin stops chaffing off like
flower petals.
want someone to creep into my childhood room and find me
cowering there underneath my bloody bedsheets.
to look at me softly with no danger in their eyes.
to show me what spring must feel like.

dad talks about writing a book and i wonder if he'll title it: how to erase your four-year-old daughter. three-in-the-morning and i'm hunched over on the floor of the kitchen like a wild animal, scratching out my face in every picture i could find from my childhood. i'm a tree falling in a forest, screaming so loud my own ears are bleeding. but it doesn't make any difference. no one is around to hear it [and god has never been listening.] someday when they find my body they'll wonder what it was that suffocated me. they'll never know how i choked on all the things i could never say.

my math teacher shows us a graph made into art, like the wheels of a bicycle. i can't move my legs. my hands shake. i'm sleepy and thirsty but don't want to drink too much and vomit.

i made a drawing too. ugly. my fingers are dark at the tips and i'm still angry. i wish it was summer.

i can't see the board well. if i relax my eyes i can make everything look soft and have no edges, pretend nothing here can hurt me. been doing it ever since i was little. it never makes anything hurt any less but it keeps the panic trapped in my throat.

the bell rings and everything becomes loud. swallow hard and it feels like i'm underwater.

shove my book in my bag and bedtime prayers begin running through my head. rise to my feet and the whiteness comes. don't know where i've gone. looks like i'm staring at the moon.

i dreamt of you last night. i was in your house looking at the floor tiles that you always wanted to show me. you were nowhere around and somehow my body made its way to the sliding door, just like your sister's did and i looked out and saw you

hanging

from a tree.

and i didn't feel anything.

i stepped outside and the snow burnt my bare feet. i took one step at a time until i was standing only a few inches away from you. your eyes were open. you had vomited on yourself. your skin was

blue.

i reached out and touched your face.
and i felt everything.

ar·ma·ged·don
/ˌärməˈgedn/

noun

- the place where yelling matches turn into fistfights and the neighbors call the cops because they think someone is being killed.
- the uprising of an angry voice belonging to an eleven-year-old girl with the same name as me. the same eyes and the same wounds. a candle pretending to be a wildfire. she will be met with holy water and cease to exist.
- the look of relief in my father's eyes as he watches the body bag being zipped shut over my face, blue. like a balloon.
- the bleeding out.
- the unbearable need for touch that won't sting and hands that won't leave bruises. the hope for and fear of trust. the wish for gentleness that won't ever be granted.
- the goodbye, and this time we all mean it.
- the kingdom come.

there's something so terrible about the cowering. no way to describe fear like that. there's something so violent about being backed into a corner, curled up in a ball with your hair caught between your teeth. all the air in the room left before your knees could hit the floor. your voice hides in your throat [and god's gonna leave you to choke.] your arms are raised like a white flag in the night and your head is tucked up behind your legs, your ten-year-old bones rattling in their frame. there's something so black-and-blue about the yelling grabbing shaking. and here comes your voice.

please

   bursting from your lungs.

sorry

   flooding from your lips.

tears pouring down your cheeks. no way out of here, no ears to catch the begging. just skin on skin. hot. angry. a stain-source for the not-so-beige [anymore] carpet.

december of senior year i pinned up sheets to cover all the mirrors so that i wouldn't have to see myself as a corpse when i tied up my hair or slipped on my jeans that were always too big. in the mornings i would wake up twice, once when the sun reached my eyes past the curtains and then again when i would come-to after collapsing on the floor, all of my blood puddling in my legs. i would drink water in sets of twenty-seven sips and sometimes puke in the hallway outside of my math class. [it only took me two weeks to relearn how to hold it in my mouth and swallow.] those were the months of coffee and cold showers and calories and crying. i blocked every number in my phone except my mom's and kathryn's. and yet there are still moments when i'm convinced that i was happiest then. sometimes i still think that living like that is all i could ever want.

i'm crawling through the bushes. i'm tearing out of the ropes
and i'm never going to make it off of my knees. i can't reach the
clean air, here it's all paint that's still drying and cigarettes. i don't
recognize the things on me as hands until the nails are dug into
my skin. strangers [almost] always taste how the bottles used to
smell and i want my mother. i'm bruising again and it's

all

over
but the
gagging.

how to be lovely at eighteen is: a body like an apology. skin that's clear for twelve hours of the day. gums and teeth burning like a wildfire. eyes with bags that carry fourteen years of saying all the right things and giving all the correct answers and a tongue that can't taste anymore. a voice that crumbles like thunder. bones that stick out like tree branches. taking cover and taking blame. caffeine pills and unanswered phone calls [and please call me back] and three a.m. fevers that end in bloodshed.

all the love in the world for boys who will only ever walk away.

no god and no heaven here. not praying for salvation or forgiveness just praying for it to be over.

the day they went on over the loudspeakers and said you had died i ran like a thief in the night. stumbled into the counselling office and everyone in the room was crying, never seen something like that before. and it was just quiet and still and there was nothing but weight. wet air. clouded.

i must've listened to *earth song* a thousand times that day. didn't know what to do. felt like i needed to call someone but when i opened my phone the only number i could type in was yours. and even now when it hurts i feel like you're the only one i could ever turn to about you dying.

the hardest part was that everyone knew, looking at me. that you and i shared a soul. and the look in their eyes felt so pathetic and so did i. whole school in a haze. felt like i had walked into a fever dream.

the social worker sat across from me and told me that it wasn't normal, to have a best friend die in high school, except i couldn't take her seriously with the eight other kids who had died in the past three years. eight of them and they were all someone's best friend, too. someone's sibling. someone's child.

that night i scratched your name into my dresser and let pills rock me to sleep. and i left my phone on loud, just in case. as if somehow you might call me and i could hear your voice again.

[and i still wait for that call.]

i dreamt of showing up in the middle of the night on his doorstep. he would let me in, no questions asked. sit me down on his couch. wrap me in a blanket and hand me a cup of tea.

he'd turn on the fireplace and lock the door [just in case.] he'd tuck my hair behind my ear and hope i wouldn't flinch and i'd say

joseph i
just
can't do this anymore

just
can't live in such a mess.

and he'd say that i'm a bruise. blood forming just below the skin with no escape. purple and black and hot to the touch. and i'd be nodding off like a child, droopy eyes and not-quite-listening.

what was it? what did he say?

a bruise. getting a little darker every day.

they rammed a tube through my nose and down my throat and pumped me with iron and glass. it still tastes like bleeding out. mary ellen came over and we watched the ants crawl from the cracks in the floorboards to the sink and back again. we painted our toenails blue before we realized they blended too well with the bruising. today my doctor ran her hands down my spine and said it looked like i was getting better. on the way home i asked to pull over and shoved my fingers down my throat to rid myself of twenty-six calories and fourteen years of hiding in my closets from monsters who preferred on top of the bed. it's hard to hide a sickness when they can hear it through the car door.

you've grabbed me by the shoulders, your thumbs digging into the wells of my collarbones and you slam me back, back, back against the cold plaster of your bathroom wall. you shake me like an angry fist, balled up newspaper, crumpling in your grasp. i can't hear what you're saying – you're screaming through your teeth. the look in your eyes reminds me of when i was younger and i watched my brother poke at a dead animal we found in the woods. only, not quite dead. angry eyes, spiteful. red through the brown. and i feel like a deer in the headlights, a dog facing the barrel of a gun. caught in the thickness of your breath, such anger and wildness here. i want to cower and retreat but there is no escaping you, not anymore. hopeless and helpless and maybe i'll spend the rest of my life in this god-forsaken house maybe i'll die and no one will find my body, maybe you'll bury me in the backyard. but all that's wishful thinking. the truth is: i could die a thousand times and still come crawling back to you, rotting off the bone. mouth open and hungry.

hurt me more.

i just feel like a bloody nose. i want the gushing to stop. every year older i turn just seems like a new scab over a wound that isn't ever going to heal. i forgot how my dad can make me feel like i've disappeared in less than five seconds. i hate it here on this rotting earth. i hate it here in this festering hellfire. i wish i could close my eyes and sleep forever, god. i wish i had never been born.

one of those nights there are monsters under my bed my eyes are throbbing and i think they'll fall out my neck feels like it's been snapped in two i'm counting the stars and the curtains are pulled tight i'm looking for god and all i see is a reflection in a mirror that is not there and that girl looking back at me is no angel.

i've bitten down my fingers on the joints and i can barely reach to switch on the lights i look around and i see ghosts dead eyes white like snow the stars are closing in now and the hunger pains pull me back to bed the monsters tuck me in and i wait wait wait for sleep or for death there would be no difference to me no i really wouldn't mind.

an inner-monologue three sleeping pills later:

i'm so scared of the dark. and what i mean by that is, i'm scared
of being alone. i'm scared of not being able to see anything. i
want to call my mom and see if she'll come pick me up, drive me
around the lake like she did before she brought me to the hospital
and they pumped my body full of saline and nasogastric formula.
the only person i've talked to in the past four days is myself and
it's getting old. everything just seems like an echo and nothing
is new. i wish i could feel something more than lonely. i wish it
were july and i were falling in love all over again. they told me
the beginning would be hard but no one said anything about this
cut-throat grief. no one said anything about crying in the grocery
store parking lot. no one said anything about wanting more than
anything to just run away.

in the presence of god i'm brought to my knees like a lamb being offered as a sacrifice and my mouth is torn open like a wound sewn shut. they're hungry. starving. can't keep my eyes open and all i hear is laughter and the sound of my own gagging. echoing like a bell choir on christmas eve. and everything's rolling over, just a dog. just an animal.

it's said that victims attract predators but i don't think that's true. i think predators are so sickeningly good at what they do that they can sniff out vulnerability in everyone. to even suggest that victims are to blame for second or third or fiftieth traumas is revolting to me. but oh well, i suppose. isn't that the kind of world we live in.

how to feel: write poetry. listen to the [forbidden] playlist. visit the churchyard. make yourself bleed. look at pictures of skinny girls. cry. watch documentaries about war and sickness. think about kathryn. hide the clumps of hair that fall out in a box under your bed. block joseph's number. remove the makeup and look at the bruises. stop taking your pills.

how to not feel: take all your pills at once.

damage control: you and i have been like this for so long we don't even notice how we've changed. it never used to be like this, you know. fist-fights and bottles of pills and words like knives. it never used to be you against me.

i'm running out into the street again and you're chasing after me like always but one day i know i'll look back over my shoulder and you won't be there anymore. it's your body pressed against mine but it won't always be like that. things like this have to come to an end.

i eat an apple slice and chew fifty times. i take a sip of water. i cough up blood. but if there's still a pounding in my chest anything's fair game. if my eyes still open the show is still on. it's how low can i get my heartrate to go. how long can i survive on water and bitter coffee i gag on due to the taste. how deep can i push the glass in. how close to 0lbs can i get.

joseph finds me in the back of the theatre, the last seat in the last row. he wraps his coat around me and it smells like old music and aftershave. he tells me i look cold and the sick girl in my head is smiling like a little kid.

later he spots me on the side of the road sucking on my lemon peels and tea leaves. he places me in the passenger seat of his rental car and begins to drive. promises he won't stop until i feel like we're far enough away.

cheap car. still, it's warm. he puts something heavy on me and my eyes are closed. i hear the soft music he always plays and wonder if the sun has set. his voice is low and he's trying to tell me something but i can't quite hear him. want to ask him what he said. what did you say. say it again. say it again.

you left and i cried through an entire choir rehearsal. jacquelyn wrapped me in her coat and drove me back to my house. she never went home that night.

the next morning she took me and my dog to these big open fields covered in snow and the sun seemed especially gentle that day, air warm like a beating heart. her cheeks were pink and she was so beautiful and soft i thought she might be some sort of angel. i couldn't feel anything except the movement of her breath and i realized that i was better off without you.

the way i told her about my brother was so blunt and unexpected that it still feels like a bruise. i thought maybe she would look at me differently after that, see me as a killer, but she was still just beautiful. still just soft.

called her one night in the bathtub with imaginary sirens blaring in my ears. wish she knew that the reason i tapped her number was because i needed someone to remind me why life was worth living. won't ever forget that girl. all the sleepless nights in my living room. days spent out in the wide-open fields. malts and movies and flower crowns. two bodies and maybe just one soul.

i've come to find that there's no room for anger in grief like this.
she woke up every morning and saw a world so angry and hateful
that she decided she'd rather slip into the night and leave all of
us behind. so my anger has nowhere to go but i guess that's how
it's always been. was that way before her and will probably be that
way for a long time. but anyway, i just wish i could let her know.
i'm not angry with her. just miss her so dearly. just think about
her, the rosiness of her cheeks and the shyness of her smile and
the warmth of her voice. just picture her glowing like a lightning
bug, like a ray of sun. just hold her close like that. want her to
know she's still being held.

i wake up and vomit. push the cat away and grind my teeth and more is coming up, seeping through. half an hour later i'm back in the sheets and i don't know what year it is. too ashamed to call. to cry. to beg, please come hold me. please come comfort me like a child. please come take care of me. a part of me died when i was small and is still lodged in my throat. please come let her out.

until i am skin and bones. and that's all there is left of me.
i will lay on the cold tile of the bathroom floor and weep into the vents. the sound will carry through the ducts to the windows in the cellar where the garden flowers will hear it and know that a homecoming is approaching.
until i am skin and bones. and that's all there is left of me.
i will search for my heart in the tangled sheets on my brother's bed in his childhood room. under the glow-in-the-dark stars where everything was ripped away from me. all those years ago when i was four-years-old and didn't know any better.
until i am skin and bones. and that's all there is left of me.
i will lay my body in the bathtub where the water turned cold hours ago. still fully clothed, pink water like a flower girl's tea. unable to drown but refusing to swim. the chain of the plug dancing between my toes. waiting but knowing i'm a girl who can never seem to make up her mind and do it [please, just do it.]
until i am skin and bones. and that's all there is left of me.

i'm learning self-preservation one papercut at a time. the person i'm trying to be hasn't changed in nineteen years and maybe i'm still a newborn. maybe i'm still new to the air and the light. i spend sundays weeping in my first communion dress on the bathroom floor, counting the stains on the ceiling. the sound of the water hits the walls and echoes through the vents and i wonder if anyone's listening. [i don't actually wonder. i know i'm alone.] the only thing i can feel is the throbbing. i look for god in the broken mirror and never thought he would be covered in blood. i throw my head back and carve the crucifixion into my hip. i tighten my fingers around my throat and hope my thoughts will drain out my eyes, foam out through my teeth. i'm learning self-preservation one blackout at a time. the person i'm trying to be died in my brother's bed and was never buried right.

i still have dreams of my teeth falling out and being forced to keep them in my mouth. chewing them down to a bloody pulp.

five minutes 'til four-in-the-morning and i left all my makeup on so i wouldn't have to see my face in the mirror. i called joseph three times [in my head] and white noise blared on the other end of the phone. i can't tell what was the cat and what was the panic. my mouth still tastes like green tea even though i scrubbed my gums until i couldn't feel them.

could be today or could be tomorrow so i guess i don't need sleep anymore.

and now i'm curled up in the pile of stuffed animals in my closet like a wild thing. i feel as small as i was then, washed up and shipwrecked. and a body like a doll.

sometimes i feel as if everyone would be better off if i were not here. when i look in the mirror i don't see anything other than a headache. people ask [gently] what the matter is and i don't know how to tell them that i'm a killer.

i'm good at finding my own grave in the darkness of my hands. i'd rather stay buried. i'm rotting, anyway.

if you breathe too heavily the floor might fall out from underneath you. i see you but it's only in the moments right before the sunrise when the world is grey and blue and you're in the garden but god has taken his fingers and smudged your face. you have no feeling anymore. i want to walk into the garden and cut everything down and lay it before your feet like a grave. pile of leaves and petals and thorns. you have no place here anymore.

lying in bed i feel like a
                              corpse.

my skin is more blue than pink.
mom tries to braid my hair but has to stop when it keeps clumping
out in her hands. i cannot stop
                                   crying.

i don't know what to say so i
                                 say nothing at all.

when i open my mouth all i do is make people
                                                sad.

i think i've been afraid of the dark my whole life. and i think i'll always be that way. even though i seem to reinvent myself every time i look in the mirror, there are some things about me that just never seem to change. i'm stubborn and i don't like to admit it, was always taught that i should be willing to do whatever i'm told no matter how i feel. but i feel deeply, painfully, entirely too much. i cry hard and i cry often. i love even when i know i shouldn't. i apologize too much and forgive too easily. i sound soft, don't i, but maybe i wish i weren't that way. it's hard to feel like a lamb in a world full of wolves.

sometimes i want to die so bad i'm afraid there might be no poems left in me.

here is what that two-in-the-morning emergency room visit taught me:

a mother holds her confessions beside her heart deep below the skin.
scared of snakes.
storms.
horror movies.
and even the thought
of
one day
having to
bury
her own
child.

the end
of
the world.

laying on the floor of the room i have lived in since i was small. i kiss the ceiling fan goodbye and throw my head back. *there is no sting.* the third handful makes itself into the armageddon. and now the last thing. the words to shove together in jumbled lines to form poems only god and i can understand. are gone now, too. my mouth is foaming and i wonder if this makes me a killer.

there is no peace in death. god did not come for me.
[i knew he wouldn't.]

my dreams are heavier than they used to be. sometimes i lay in bed and [if i close my eyes] i can cut out all the hurt and then all that's left is skin and bones. i think back to over the summer and imagine what it would have been like if you were there. cold on the floor of the shower but then you could have been there to pull me out. i think of now and imagine what it would be like if you were here. cold on the floor of the shower but then you would be here to check for a pulse and scream for my mother. i don't think of you stopping me. i only think of you waiting with me until i'm sleeping.

god is looking down on us like a pile of dead bodies and all we have to offer is *i'msorryi'msorryi'msorryi'msorry* and there is no fear of death just what comes after and

please god, let it be soft.

i'm sorry i make you feel: guilty. neither of us are surprised that it's seven years later and i'm still the one apologizing. after all, you raised me on my knees. i know you can't look at me. [i know you probably don't even want to.] you're god, aren't you. but it's strange how your entire empire was about to come crashing down as soon as i opened my mouth. i don't hesitate in who i pray to now and my voice doesn't tremble. there are ten commandments and none of them talk about keeping what my brother did a secret for the sake of the family's image. so go ahead, burn me at the stake. douse me in gasoline and declare me a heathen. my kingdom will come. and so will yours.

i guess i was just failed over and over. hard not to take that on myself. little girl with bruised up legs who doesn't like talking about it and yet at the same time says far too much without even trying. i look at pictures of myself from kindergarten. fifth grade. middle school. even senior year and i. just think. about how many people saw me. saw it. and said nothing. did nothing. when i couldn't do anything for myself.

it took me nineteen years to piece everything together but it still happened. you were probably hoping that it would all stay shattered for me. looking back it isn't hard to tell why you fought me every step of the way. each time i would open my mouth you knew i was growing closer and closer to finding it. you were scared, rightfully so. you were just hoping that you had beaten me down enough to keep me quiet.

you hadn't.

the truth crashed into me all at once. and then it swelled on top of me and i choked and spit from underneath it. it left no room for air. and the more i looked at it the more i realized that it wasn't my first time seeing it. remembering it was just remembering the last time i remembered it. it had been there all along. tucked behind my shoulder blades, just out of reach. i found it and suddenly everything made sense.

i finally knew what you were really trying to shut me up about.

nothing could have prepared me for you killing yourself.

hard to know i couldn't tell anyone even if i wanted to, even if i tried. they made me into a shipwreck and all i am is sharp and rotting from the inside out. and that's all anyone ever sees and that's all i'll ever be.

wrapped so tightly around myself that blood stopped flowing years ago and i can't look anyone in the eyes for too long or i might start to come undone.

that would be the end of me, you know. i've saved the best for last and as it turns out, it's just my crumbling. decaying. gone as quietly as i came.

all of my life people have been telling me to fix myself. to pick up all these broken pieces and fit them back together. get it together. get ahold of myself. *get a grip*. and i guess they just don't understand i guess they will never understand. that when your entire head is shattered as a child. it's hard to know how to put it back together. and some of the pieces seem to be missing. left on the couch in my grandmother's house. and in my brother's childhood bed under his glow-in-the-dark stars. and in the dead-end corner of the shower in the downstairs bathroom. in all the places where hands were something more than hands and my body was lost to hunger. in all the places my mind left my rotting shell to escape the feelings of filth and shame. in all the places i was cut open and gutted like a fruit. my insides pouring out onto the floor. i am a pile of sea glass. every edge i ever had has been softened by time and unwanted touch. i don't fit together anymore. too many pieces are missing. the ones that are here don't match. and how am i to ever know. all the places where my pieces were left. if some days it's hard to even recall my name.

can't find a way to let our bodies stay here. your fingers haven't even brushed my skin yet and i am already turning pink and peeling. you're the songs from my childhood and i haven't heard anything but my own choking and heaving in years. what are you doing here. *don't you know i ruin everything i touch.* wild. feral. stupid in love. i want to tell you everything i could never say but the only words i know are

   leave me.

         and,

            i'm sorry.

i just knew not to tell i just knew. i loved my brother and nothing else about it mattered.

i will never understand.

i cannot imagine choosing one child over the other i cannot imagine turning my back and closing my eyes like hide-and-seek, pretending nothing was wrong i cannot imagine playing all the games and telling all the lies until i really truly believed it was all real.

perfect little life we had, huh. like a house of dolls.

and.

i want you to know that if you ever wake up one day and decide that you finally love me, i'll still be waiting outside in the rain for you. and when you open the door i'll just run to you; it'll be that simple.

and i promise i'll be good and gentle and won't ever make you hurt.

'cause i'm still a child, mom. still a baby left out here. and my cheeks are still pink and soft and i cry at loud noises and when i'm alone in the dark. and you've left me out here for nineteen years like a wild thing and i'm still here.

still hoping. still waiting.

knees numb on the concrete and every prayer is still for you, the ones you taught me to say before bedtime. and i don't think i'll ever leave this place. someday maybe it'll just be a pile of bones here.

guess that's how it is. really, truly rotting for you.

baby pink shirt with ponies on it. braids running down my shoulders like handlebars. disney princess lip gloss from christmas that tastes like grapes and sugar smeared messily across my mouth like paint. peach-colored skin, burnt slightly from the sun, tender to the touch. bright white sneakers and teeth, beaming smile. [the dentist said no cavities.] dollhouses and stuffed animals and cd's playing nursery rhymes and pillow forts and sleepovers and

i was just a child.
how could you.

the truth is i will always have more poems to write about mom & dad.

i would never admit it to you but. i miss you like a body misses a limb. it doesn't stop hurting until i'm finally drowning in sleep. but ever since you left i've been waking up in a panic. wide-eyed like an animal. screaming for my mother. i am a creature of the night. i am leaking apologies.

there must be a soft place for me. somewhere, i just haven't found it yet. there must be a place with no throbbing or ache, no metal or mold. i can't remember for sure but it seems like i've always been in this unsafe place. the place where christmas lights make me uneasy and i vomit in the mornings after i sleep in my brother's room. if there's one thing i've learned [other than how to be quiet] it's that seas can't stay low forever. they rise. they flood. they make things clean.

it tastes like blood and it hurts so badly. there's only one place in the world where the stinging would stop. if you're wondering what it was that tore me up so much inside, so am i. how did i last a whole lifetime in that house and why is freedom shrinking me down. why can't i walk anymore. why can i only crawl. it tastes like a black-out and waking up heaving. please don't leave me here to rot.

please don't leave me here to rot.

cali is. the sun. sand. and sea. and you may choke on it. but the thing is, there is nothing bad to remember. you are a girl and you will always be a girl. it will always be dangerous for you to walk out alone on the street. and in cali that is no different but the raging fear is less. and you feel it. it is a blinding feeling, to feel free like that. your bones don't rattle against each other and your skin doesn't shrivel up, white. pale. drowsy. there are tears in cali but there is no sorrow. beautiful people dance beautiful dances and you're pulled up onto your feet, and a stinging in your chest doesn't even stop you. your head doesn't pound and your ears don't ring. there is only ever music to be heard. all the stars you lost can be found right above you. you just have to be willing to look up. your body is *your* body. and it's somehow beautiful despite all the scars. cali is the place to heal. more of a cure than any drug has ever been.

i have to tell myself i'm not made of paper anymore even though
i rip and tear – i have to remember this body is made of flesh and
i am inherently tender, i fall off the bone. i bruise and i bleed, it's
just my nature. nothing i could've done to be this way. when i set
myself on fire i don't disintegrate into thin ash i boil and blister
and peel. my rotting takes time. and i can't fold myself up and tuck
myself away into the cracks of the floorboards and i can't throw
myself into the wind and fly away with the leaves but

this skin
is

warm.
balmy.
gentle.

and underneath there's a steady, unfaltering beating.

and my eyes are soft.
and my hands are soft.
and my cheeks are soft and the crook of my neck

soft.
warm.

and more than just me can live here in this

soft.
warm.

i've started saying *i love you* and the scary part is i don't exactly know what that means. i know what it used to mean. i don't have to think hard at all to remember knocked over traffic cones and snowstorms in mid-july. i'm not sure how to navigate this new kind of love. i'm so used to driving at night, the streets look different in the light of the sun. all i know is i'm crashing into you because i'm only good at falling apart. but so far there's been no collapse. i don't know how to read the map in my hands and i have no compass other than the one thumping in my chest but for some reason i know it's gonna be alright for me, for us. anywhere new will be better than where i came from.

the importance of falling apart:
the body is like a garden and sometimes the winter is harsh and the spring is even harsher and when we're flooded out and then dried up like a desert. what can we do other than rip up all our weeds and our roots and start over. we still have this strange place of our own full of cakey dirt and rocks and the sun always comes again, even when we feel like everything and everybody in the world has left us.

sophomore year of high school i chopped off all of my hair and when my aunt saw me she told me that sometimes when we feel like everything is falling to shit we have to make some sort of drastic change and i feel that now, sitting on the bathroom floor as i snip off my bangs for the millionth time, wondering if this time will finally be the last. [don't think it ever will be.]

when i learned what happened with my father i looked jack straight in the eyes and told him that i needed to be held like a child and finally for the first time in my life i felt like i let go of everything and it didn't matter because he was there holding onto me and i wasn't going anywhere. it was an ugly cry, the kind where my breaths came in hiccups and my makeup ran down my face like i was a circus clown but there in his arms when the room finally stopped spinning i felt the most at peace i've felt in a long, long time.

so i have to remember that falling apart is okay. in the end all my pieces will still be there and i'll always fit back together again, somehow.

you're teaching me to walk through the dark and i've been blind for years. i've written you a journal full of love letters that i keep hidden under my left collarbone in plain sight. i have so many things to tell you and no tongue, no teeth. how your hands pull me out from under the floorboards and wipe the blood from my cheeks. how every shooting star and 11:11 is saved for you. i don't remember falling in love. i only remember waking up beside you and knowing morning had come. sometimes when you'd drive me through the night i would close my eyes and pretend that you were finally bringing me home.

there was a time when god had me convinced that i was really no soft thing. that all the years of being tethered to the bed and having my legs burned with rods that were heated on the stove had worn away at my wild warmth. but i have learned to look at myself in mirrors with my heart instead of the eyes of my father. no devil-child here.
look in the glass and see.
girl.
gentle as the morning.
i have not been sharpened. i have not been carved into a blade. i've changed but only in the sense of the petals of a flower soaking in ginger tea and nineteen year's time. things have torn away at my outer layers but the thing i have come to realize is: i am the *tenderness caressing tenderness*. there is nothing else to find here. so maybe we should all stop looking.

all my life
you tried to convince me that i was just sick that i would just never
understand that i was just so inherently broken that nothing would
ever fix me and nothing would ever be okay for me
and i think that you were foolish.

what did you
think
was going to happen?

you couldn't control me forever.

maybe you expected that i would die before i grew up and left.
[i think a part of me expected that, too.]

i guess we were both wrong.

and now i know.
i wasn't ever the sick one.

somehow i am still able to look to the skies and thank god for the morning. i need to be able to appreciate that in its entirety. that after all of the night i can still be grateful for the sun, no matter how late it rises. i could be as sour as the lemons they squeezed into my foaming mouth and yet here i am. as sweet and pure as the day i was born.

to: jack
re: a playlist i made for you

it's a jumble of a bunch of good stuff and doesn't make much sense
but that's kind of what it's like to love someone. loving all of them
and not needing a reason why.

we are the flower girls of the wild gardens after the forest fires. we tie and untie ribbons around our wrists and count the days we can see the moon from under the sun. we do not fear dirt. we know we have come from it. some days we are growing and some days we are crawling. we don't wonder if water will reach us. we cry enough tears that we may drown. the flames could come again any moment of any day, but we are ready. teeth sharpened and fists curled. and yet, we could never be unsoft.

i did not grow up in my house. i grew up everywhere else. in elizabeth's childhood bed, listening to an audiobook of *the secret garden* and falling asleep to the rhythm of her breaths. in the hallway outside my math class where i stumbled after the bell, pressed up against the lockers, fifty hours into a fast and burning out like a candle in the night. waking up to a familiar face looking sad and unsure, realizing he followed me out, even though i told him i would be fine to walk myself. in the little office in the arts center, playing with the toys on the desk, saying nothing and everything all at once and for the first time in my life feeling like someone was listening, like maybe i wasn't a ghost, wasn't ever a ghost and it was really just the people who treated me that way who were to blame. in a hammock under the mid-august sun. clinging to jack like a child, an abandoned animal. waking to the sound of music. coming undone. i was not raised right and yet here i am. nineteen years later and. i know i'm still very much a child but that doesn't mean that i've done it all alone. so lonely it's debilitating and yet. on the rare occasion that i open my eyes and look around. i realize that i've been surrounded by people, by love, this whole time.

- thank you, to those who helped raise me when no one else would.

if i have one thing to say to you, it's that you were wrong. about everything.

i'm going to keep growing and learning and speaking my truth and there's nothing you can do to stop me.

you thought you could cripple me with fear. you thought you could burn me out. you thought you could convince me that i was the one who was born a monster. that it was all me. all my fault.

you were wrong.

you tried to turn me into a ghost. you tried to keep me but you couldn't. you tried to get me to believe that no one would ever give me love that didn't hurt, so i would always have to settle for yours.

and you were wrong.

i just wish i could show you. what it's like to be buried in the sand for nineteen years and then to suddenly be unearthed by a tidal wave. beautiful and terrifying. i wish i could show you how it felt. when your warmth spread across my skin like a wildfire. i want to take you by your shoulders and show you what it's like to crash into love. so gently. tenderly. softly. i want to throw my hands in the air towards the fields and the hills and the sun and the sky and admit to you with my voice caught in my throat that you've given all this to me. made me a whole new world where there is no night. wish i could tell you, wish you could know. how you're the morning.

you are the new day.

lying together, [half asleep.] your arm underneath my neck, my legs draped over yours. your face is glowing like the moon through my half-closed eyelids and your breaths come steadily like a first snow. you're the warm summer sun and i cling to you like a child. your fingertips brush my face and i begin to unravel. you seep into my wildfire of a heart and i am sated. and oh my love, i come undone for you.

oh my love, i am made soft.

just want you to know
that

you raised me with
bitterness
&
rage
&
guilt
&
hate

and i turned out so
unapologetically
soft
&
sweet
&
warm
&
wild.

i write love poems in my sleep and tuck them away behind my eyelids for the morning. and when i wake i am soft and gentle with stars dotting my cheeks. some days i almost believe i could cry them out for you but in the end i never do. there are some kinds of love so great that there are no words to explain them.

and i wake to the echoes of music. wrapped in your embrace and the flush of a sunrise; i imagine spring has come. naked – draped in sunlight. you say my name and i begin to weep. as if i am hearing it just now for the first time.

i'll be screaming it to the heavens, 'til the day i die:

that boy is the sun
and
his softness raises the morning.

maybe the worst part is that everyone who was supposed to protect me, didn't.

look at how beautiful i turned out, in spite of you.

the fever broke. we can rest now. sometimes we have to bruise before we can heal. [and i still believe in you. and i still believe in us.] our pinky promises are hung on the string lights tucked between our eyelashes and

> i still love you
>
> > more and more.
> >
> > > every day.

this is us: reaching out our arms. digging into each other's hearts. into the good and the dark and the wild. loving each other there. rocking each other to sleep. and i am softer now. knowing you'll be there in the morning.

so.
please,
don't
go.

when my grip loosens and the color returns to my knuckles. when the day is folding in on itself and the darkness is unravelling over the ground. let me find rest in the quiet.

and in the morning. let me rise up singing.

kathryn. i have so many things left to say to you and i don't think i'll ever be at peace with what happened junior year but i just want you to know that i'm sorry, i'm so sorry that i didn't believe you and that no one else believed you, i'm so sorry that none of us were there, it would've taken one person, just one, to step in and do something and we all failed you. and everyone else may say otherwise but i'll always believe that we could've saved you. [i could've saved you.] people in that school liked to pretend that they cared but we both know that test scores and titles were all they were ever concerned with, i hope they remember you and hate themselves. and kathryn i think of you every day i look at your picture i remember you zooming through the halls on your heelys and throwing your batons in the air and singing your songs and dancing your dances and i remember how your voice sounded, how you smelled like flowers. and i don't know what i believe in or what became of you but i like to think that you're somewhere softer now, with people who deserve you and all your goodness. and every time i look up at the stars i say your name even if it's just in my head and i want you to know that, that we still say your name like you can hear us. won't ever stop saying your name. won't ever let you fade into the quiet. you were one of the hardest lessons i've ever had to learn but i want you to know that i am a better, kinder, softer person for knowing you. we all are.

and my love, oh my love.
i've finally dreamt of it.

a quiet afternoon on a soft day
                        [thank god]
                                        in the spring.

somewhere in a field of flowers where the sun won't set.
surrounded by all the lives we've touched.
all the people we've loved.

i'm guided out into the light and see you.
and you see me.
and we were
                blind
                        before this moment.

i walk myself down the aisle.
i was never my father's to give away.

i meet you where the sun leans down to kiss the earth
and finally we set the seal upon the promise i've believed in all
along:

that i was made for loving you.

i was made for loving you.

it's gentle here. we've reached the edge and you're done crying. your face is soft and we can already smell the wooden crates. we're walking on clouds here. the sky is blue and white and every color we've ever touched. every color we've ever felt. i can't feel my hands anymore. we know we're in the sky. we're unafraid. i've carried you all the way here, to the bridge, to the door. to the crossroads. here we will be stripped of our clothes. stripped of our skin. stripped of everything we ever knew except for the things we could only acknowledge in our sleep. the wind is singing songs from our childhood. god isn't here. and, god is everywhere. i look down and see nothing. my eyes are gone. everything is gone and we're filled with the warmth and grief of all the faces who have faded away. all the lives we've touched. all the people we've loved. and before we can even ask if we're welcome in the stars, before we can try to walk across the gap to freedom.

god lifts us up.
and he carries us home.

About the Author

Mee Eun is a 19-year-old Korean-adopted American writer whose horrific childhood has inspired her to finally break her silence and share her story through poetry. She attended a single semester of college before deciding to leave and seek more intensive therapy to work through her trauma. She is a lover of art, music, and helping others. She was hesitant to write and release i wish i wouldn't have survived, but ultimately determined that her voice and experiences were worth sharing, both to inform and to provide hope.

Printed in the United States
By Bookmasters